Bilingual Edition
READING POWER
Edición Bilingüe

Extreme Machines

Monster Trucks

Camionetas gigantes

Scott P. Werther

The Rosen Publishing Group's
PowerKids Press™ & Buenas Letras™
New York

1

Published in 2003 by The Rosen Publishing Group, Inc.
29 East 21st Street, New York, NY 10010
Copyright © 2003 by The Rosen Publishing Group, Inc.

First Bilingual Edition 2003
First Edition in English 2002

Book Design: Victoria Johnson
Text: Scott P. Werther
Photo Credits: Cover © AFP/Corbis; pp. 4–5, 9, 13, 14–15, 17–21 © Bigfoot 4x4 Inc.; pp. 6–7 © Watson/The Image Works; pp. 10–11 © J. Froscher/The Image Works

Thanks to Bigfoot 4X4, Inc.

Werther , Scott P
Monster Trucks/Camionetas gigantes/Scott P. Werther ; traducción al español: Spanish Educational Publishing
p. cm. — (Extreme Machines)
Includes bibliographical references and index.
ISBN 0-8239-6891-X (lib. bdg.)
1. Monster Trucks—Juvenile literature. [1. Monster Trucks 2.Trucks. 3. Spanish Language Materials—Bilingual.] I. Title.
TG106.K63 T48 2001
624'.5—dc21

                                        2001000599

Manufactured in the United States of America

Contents _____

_____ Contenido

This is a monster truck. Monster trucks have very large tires. These trucks race and do special tricks.

Ésta es una camioneta gigante.
Tiene llantas muy grandes.
Con estas camionetas se corren
carreras y se hacen maniobras
especiales.

The tires of monster trucks can be as tall as ten feet (3m).

Las llantas de las camionetas gigantes pueden medir 10 pies (3m).

Monster trucks are very heavy.
They use very large engines
to help them move.

Las camionetas gigantes
son muy pesadas.
Necesitan un motor
muy grande.

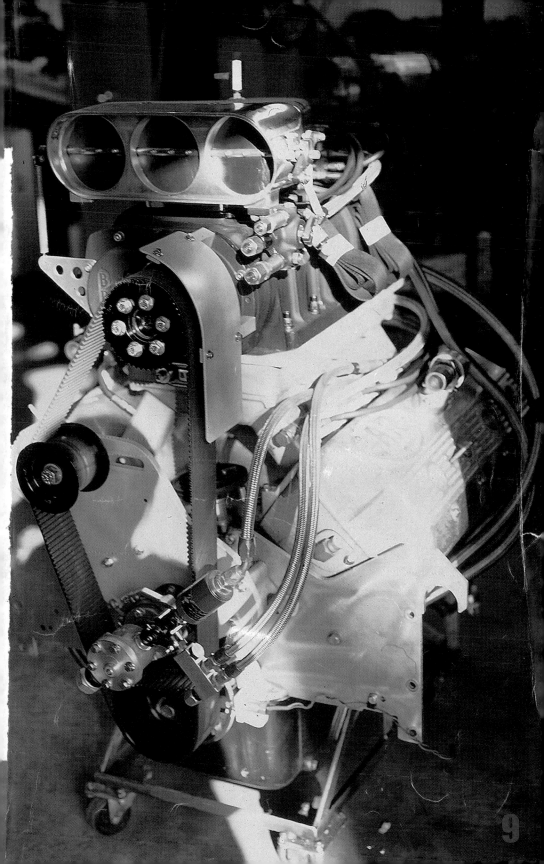

The body of a monster truck lifts up. This makes it easier for people to fix the engine.

La carrocería se puede levantar.
De este modo es más fácil
arreglar el motor.

Monster trucks use special springs and shock absorbers. The springs and shock absorbers make riding in a monster truck very smooth.

Las camionetas gigantes tienen muelles y amortiguadores especiales. Gracias a ellos es muy cómodo viajar en estas camionetas.

Amortiguador

Shock
Absorber

Most monster trucks are very colorful. They have fancy paint jobs.

Muchas camionetas gigantes
son muy coloridas.
Están decoradas con diseños bonitos.

Drivers wear hard helmets
to keep safe. They also wear
seat belts.

———————————————

Los conductores se ponen
un casco duro para protegerse
la cabeza.
También usan el cinturón de
seguridad.

Monster trucks can do tricks. They can even drive over other cars.

Las camionetas gigantes pueden
hacer maniobras especiales.
Hasta pueden andar encima
de otros autos.

These monster trucks are racing each other. Monster trucks are as fun to watch as they are to drive.

Estas camionetas están
corriendo una carrera.
¡Es tan divertido mirarlas
como manejarlas!

Glossary

body (**bahd**-ee) the main part of a monster truck

engine (**ehn**-juhn) a machine that changes fuel into motion and power

helmet (**hehl**-miht) a covering to protect the head

seat belt (**seet behlt**) a strap used to hold people steady in their seats

shock absorber (**shahk** uhb-**sorb**-uhr) a device that helps make a car or truck ride smoother

springs (**sprihngz**) a coil of metal or plastic that returns to its original shape after it is pulled or pushed

tires (**tyrz**) thick, round rubber coverings that go around the wheels of a vehicle

tricks (**trihks**) clever acts of skill

Glosario

amortiguadores (los) sistema de resortes que ayudan a que un viaje en auto o camioneta sea más cómodo

carrocería (la) parte principal de un auto o camioneta

casco (el) protector duro para la cabeza

cinturón de seguridad (el) correa que sujeta a una persona a su asiento

llanta (la) cubierta gruesa de goma que se pone alrededor de las ruedas de un vehículo

maniobra (la) prueba difícil

muelle (el) resorte de metal o plástico que vuelve a su forma inicial después de estirarlo o apretarlo

motor (el) máquina que da potencia a otra máquina

Resources / Recursos

Here are more books to read about monster trucks:
Otros libros que puedes leer sobre camionetas gigantes:

Monster Machines
by Caroline Bingham
Dorling Kindersley Publishing (1998)

Monster Trucks
by James Koons
Capstone Press (1996)

Web sites
Due to the changing nature of Internet links, PowerKids Press
has developed an online list of Web sites related to the subject
of this book. This site is updated regularly. Please use this link to
access the list:

Sitios web
Debido a las constantes modificaciones en los sitios de Internet,
PowerKids Press ha desarrollado una guía on-line de sitios
relacionados al tema de este libro. Nuestro sitio web se
actualiza constantemente. Por favor utiliza la siguiente dirección
para consultar la lista:

http://www.buenasletraslinks.com/chl/tmb

Word count in English: 137
Número de palabras en español: 134

Index

Índice